Pivotal Plots

A Quick Guide To Writing Well

P.S. Wells

Pegwood Publishing

Title: How to Pen Pivotal Plots

By P.S. Wells

Subjects: 1. Authorship Reference (Books)

2. Writing Skill Reference (Books)

3. Creativity (Books)

Key Words: How to write, character, conflict, character-driven story, creativity, fiction writing, write story, write fiction

ISBN Ebook: 979-8-9879809-6-5

ISBN Paperback: 979-8-9879809-7-2

Published by Pegwood Publishing

Roanoke IN 46783

Contents

Chapter One

On Your Mark, Get Set, Write

B efore you begin writing, save time and effort by knowing these four things.

1. What is your idea?

2. Who is your audience?

3. How does your idea, message, or story benefit your audience?

4. What is the best method to share your idea to your particular audience?

Every project begins with an idea.

First, decide what is the story or message, lesson or insight you want to share?

Hone the idea down to a laser point. The tighter the focus the better you stay on target. The tighter the message the easier for your reader to follow where you take them.

Do not be intimidated to find others have written on the same topic. You have your own slant, your own experience, your own insight which is unique to you. There is always room in the market for fresh ways of thinking on a familiar topic. Your voice will be different from other authors.

Put considerable thought into how you will present your idea in a unique fashion.

What is your idea?

Second, you have an idea, message, or story you want to share. The question is, who do you want to share your message with?

Before you begin, clarify exactly who you are speaking to. This is as important as dialing a specific number when you make a phone call.

No project – outside God's Word – is for everyone. Who is your target audience? Who is interested in receiving your message?

Age, education level, ethnicity, faith, gender, hobbies, interests, and profession are among the considerations when you define your audience. Academics, artists, and athletes each have unique jargon and terminology as do zoning specialists, zoologists, and zoo keepers. Bestselling author, Jerry Jenkins, pictured his mother sitting across the desk as he wrote his novels. She represented the audience he had in mind for the stories he told.

How specific can you be when you describe your audience?

· *The Ten Best Decisions A Single Mom Can Make* is practical help and tangible tips for solo parents ages 24 to 45, eager to create a healthy and successful family.

· *Slavery in the Land of the Free* informs intermediate and high school students about human trafficking in the United States.

· Geared for four to eight-year-olds, *The Girl Who Wore Freedom* is the true story of five-year-old Dany who was given Lifesavers and liberty on D-Day.

Writing to children is completely different from communicating with teens which differs from sharing with adults. Generally speaking, the vocabulary that appeals to women is not the same as the descriptions that resonate with men. While the words in a toddler's board book are chosen as carefully as the text for a novel, the volume is exceedingly fewer. Knowing your audience guides your vocabulary level and the length of your project in the same way you craft a conversation with an industry professional far differently than you prepare to talk with a child.

Third, how does your idea, message, or story benefit your audience? Why would your reader trade their hard-earned funds to purchase your project? Why would someone invest their limited time to read your writing?

In other words, what take-home value do you provide?

Types of take-home value writers offer include

- entertainment

- education

- guidance

- humor

- how-to instruction

- inspiration

- information

When you pen a project to be viewed and consumed by others, you create an exchange. You expect your audience to read your writing. Your audience expects you will make the experience of reading your work worthwhile. To keep your end of the agreement, clarify the benefit you plan to provide. Purposefully and generously give your audience abundant take-home value.

Fourth, once you know your audience and the take-home value you will provide to that audience, it's time to decide on the best vehicle to convey your message. There are myriad ways for a writer to communicate including

apps
articles
books
children's books
curriculum
greeting cards
novel
screenplay

song

web content

As writers, we have myriad formats to connect with readers. When you know your target audience, and the take-home value you want to deliver, then consider what format will be the most effective to share your message. You have plenty of options.

A writer has one job to do and that is to elicit an emotional response in the reader. When you write a book or want to improve a story, begin with plot. How can you use plot to elicit emotion within your reader?

Chapter Two

Plot Is

You have a story to share, a message to tell through writing. There are foundational aspects to writing well including a well-crafted plot.

Essentials for a powerful story are

1. a character the reader cares about

2. a very great life-changing, world-impacting need the character must achieve

3. a great obstacle between the character we care about and the character's life-changing, world-impacting need

Critical elements for a compelling, memorable story that works include

- Pivotal Plots

- Memorable Characters

- Sensational Settings

- Dynamic Dialog

- Point of View

Plot comprises what characters do and why they do it.
Within the construct of story, plot is the main events presented as an interrelated, though not necessarily chronological, sequence. Well-crafted plot propels the protagonist on a compelling and transformational adventure. Plot springs from and is intertwined with the character's strengths and weaknesses, needs and desires, as well as choices and dreams.

To build your plot:

Amplify: Threaten your character's basic needs, the ones that support existence. Drop complex characters into challenging circumstances and how will they respond?

Intensify: Complicate their physical needs with longings of the heart including acceptance, belonging, connection, relationship, and love.

Magnify: What choices will your characters make and what are the consequences of those actions? How are others impacted by the actions of your characters? Who is harmed if the character makes a good choice? Who is hurt if the character fails? What choice does the character make when his deepest desire is at odds with the greater good?

Plot is conflict.

Chapter Three

Nine Basic Plots

There are nine basic plots. Distill every story and you will find a version of one or more of these.

Character versus

- self

- God

- their destiny

- another character

- environment

- society or culture

- machine

- situation or circumstance

- the unknown

What plot categories do your favorite titles and films fit into? What do the nine basic plots look like in stories that remain in your memory?

As an example, see how these plots are central to these stories.

- Character versus self: Scrooge in *A Christmas Carol*

- Character versus God: Jonah in the Bible book of *Jonah*

- Character versus their destiny: Luke Skywalker in *Star Wars*

- Character versus another character: Jean Valjean and Javert in *Les Miserables*

- Character versus environment: The crew of the Andrea Gail in *The Perfect Storm*

- Character versus society or culture: Anne and the Jewish community in *Anne Frank: Diary of a Young Girl*, and Corrie ten Boom and her family in *The Hiding Place*

- Character versus machine: John Henry versus the steam drill in Disney's *John Henry,* and astronaut Dave versus the computer HAL in *2001: A Space Odyssey*

- Character versus situation or circumstance: The Good Samaritan told by Jesus in the book of Matthew

- Character versus the unknown: The characters of the *Star Trek* series as they boldly go where no man has gone before

What other stories fit into these categories?

What category does your story fall into?

Chapter Four

Tenth Plot

For a better story, use the powerful tenth plot. Add a ticking clock or a ticking bomb. Limit the amount of time your character has to achieve their big need.

- If the Avengers cannot close the wormhole in time, the alien chitauri will take over the world.

- If Joseph doesn't get his family away from Bethlehem quickly, baby Jesus will be killed by Herod's soldiers.

- If the scientists at NASA cannot figure a way to extend a limited amount of oxygen, the astronauts on Apollo 13 will die.

Increase tension by using the time constraint to force the main character to choose between two bad choices.

Not:

- Will Stevie pass his spelling test?

- Will Ellie get a date to the prom?

Instead:

- Will Steve Rogers protect America from nuclear destruction?

- Will Cinderella get to the ball and meet Prince Charming or perish in slavish obscurity?

In the *Captain America* film, the newly created Captain America must choose between two conflicting options. If he crashes into the ocean with the armed nuclear bomb, he saves New York but loses his life and that rare chance of a life of true love with Peggy. If Steve Rogers chooses a life with Peggy and saves himself while New York disappears in a mushroom cloud, the death of those people will be on his conscious as well as the knowledge that he did the selfish thing at the cost of the lives of others. Though alive, he would despise himself, lose Peggy's love and respect, and live tortured which is no life at all. With either choice, he loses something important.

Cinderella has a tight window of time provided by her Fairy Godmother to win the heart of the prince. If she succeeds, Cinderella earns the potential of true love and freedom. If she fails, she is condemned to a lifetime of drudgery with her cruel stepmother and stepsisters. Her fate must be decided in the short hours before the clock strikes midnight.

Chapter Five

Eleventh Plot

To rachet the suspense in your story even more, weave in more than one basic plot. In *Lord of the Rings*, J.R.R. Tolkien layered the epic tale with multiple plots.

Frodo versus

- self, battling fear, exhaustion, and injuries

- his destiny as he would rather remain in the peaceful Shire, thank you very much

- another character from Black Riders to Gollum to Sauron

- environment from spiders the size of Buicks to orcs to crossing the Misty Mountains

- society or culture in foreign territories including Old Forest and Barrows Down

- situation or circumstance, tempted always by the lure and draw of the dangerous ring he carries

- the unknown which is all around the Hobbit as he travels to places he's never seen and encounters dangers he never imagined

Tolkien added the pressure of the ticking clock. Supported by the nine members of the Company of the Ring, Frodo must complete his impossible quest before time runs out. If Frodo and his fellow Hobbits cannot throw the ring into the Fires of Mount Doom in Mordor before Sauron amasses his power, the evil lord will rule Middle Earth.

Tolkien's epic stories have endured time and generations. His skillful creativity and writer's imagination are showcased in the multi-layered plots of his works.

Which of the nine basic plots exist in your story? Where can you add additional plots to complicate the choices your character must make? How can you limit the character's amount of time to solve the problem and achieve their goal?

Chapter Six

Plots in Chasing Sunrise

In my novel, *Chasing Sunrise,* I layered several plots and added a ticking bomb in the form of a destructive category 5 hurricane bearing down on the island and our favorite characters. Reading *Chasing Sunrise,* readers find character Michael Northington versus

- Self as Michael struggles under intense feelings of guilt

- God with a conscious that knows good from evil but is not familiar with his Creator

- Destiny when he leaves the military but is called back to solve the murder of his friend

- Another character as he strives to outmaneuver international criminals

- Environment as he dodges sharks during a water rescue

- Society or culture as he learns to live on an island

- Machine as critical equipment fails

- Situation or circumstance when choosing to disobey orders to save lives

- Unknown because our hero doesn't know the identity of the killers

- The ticking clock looms as Hurricane Hugo, a category 5 storm, bears down on all Michael Northington holds dear on the island of St. Croix

Which of the nine basic plots exist in your story? Where can you add additional plots to complicate the choices your character must make? How can you limit the character's amount of time to solve the problem and achieve their goal?

Chapter Seven

Plot and Point of View

The plot is fueled by conflict, and conflict is often a matter of point of view. If your chapter lacks suspense and when a story is not working, try changing the POV.

Consider who in the story has the most at stake.

In *The Patent,* I took the weakest chapter out of the hero's view. This scene only had two characters – the good guy and the not good guy. This was the point of no return, the event that launched everything that came after until the final resolution 400 pages later. This was the moment when the bad guy made his move against our protagonist. From the good guy's POV, he just had to be there and get got. The passive victim.

But the villain became three-dimensional as I scoped out the landscape from his calculating eye. Our friendly friends and neighbors were suddenly dangerous if they noticed him. Every movement was orchestrated to get the dirty deed done without a witness. To commit the witnessless crime.

This chapter became one of my favorites when I shifted the point of view. Surprisingly, the person with the most to lose for this snapshot in time was not the one being kidnapped, but the kidnapper. Looking much different from the locals, the bad guy had to do what he came to do without raising suspicion or being noticed. If he were caught, he would spend his life in prison. Changing the POV in this chapter provided the suspense that keeps readers turning pages.

When a chapter lacks that page-turning depth, rewrite from the POV of another character. When a story or chapter is flat, reconsider who truly has the most at risk. Plot is enhanced when each chapter is written from the point of view of the character who has the most to lose.

Chapter Eight

Add Suspense

Add suspense to the plot by dripping key information to the reader.

Suspense compels readers to wonder what will happen next.

Tension is built when an author resists the urge to dump a lot of information on the reader at one time. Go ahead and pour all the information on the page if that helps you write. Where an abundance of background, details, and behind-the-scenes peeks is dumped in one place, take out the bits that are not immediately necessary. Strategically and slowly reveal what the characters do and the vital why behind their choices.

Robert Louis Stevenson gave a splendid example in the opening of *Treasure Island.*

I remember him as if it were yesterday, as he came plodding to the inn door, his sea chest following behind him in a hand-barrow–a tall, strong, heavy, nut-brown man, his tarry pigtail falling over the shoulder of his soiled blue coat, his hands ragged and scarred, with black, broken nails, and the saber cut across one cheek, a dirty, livid white. I remember him looking round the cover and whistling to

himself as he did so, and then breaking out in that old sea song that
he sang so often afterward: Fifteen men on the dead man's chest—
Yo-ho-ho, and a bottle of rum!"

- Why is a sailor on land?

- What is in the chest?

- What brings a sailor to an inn?

- Why are his fingernails black?

- How did he get a saber scar on his face?

For generations, readers have been spurred by these questions to read to the end, confident the author who penned this paragraph to hint at these questions will answer them. Kidnapped is a classic in part due to skillful plotting by a creative author.

Rather than an information dump, important information can be dropped like a surprise bomb in dialog. "Did you know she resigned today?" A single sentence can provide a crucial plot point without the use of an entire scene to show the same event. Readers read to be surprised by plot twists.

Keep the reader asking questions and the reader will keep turning pages. With each added insight, as the saying goes, the plot thickens. Unanswered questions, particularly as they affect the character the reader cares about, create anticipation.

Plot is deepened by the slow, and calculated dispensing of critical knowledge about the characters, what they do, and why.

Chapter Nine

Plot in Three Acts

Within the construct of narrative fiction, plot is the strategic presentation of interrelated main events. When crafting your story, sometimes having a template to guide where to include key aspects is helpful to the full development of your plot.

One popular outline is the three-act story. In his 1979 book, *Screenplay: The Foundations of Screenwriting*, Syd Field outlined the three parts as Setup, Confrontation, and Resolution. In this format, the tale generally fits into three parts. The first and third sections are a quarter in length to equal half of the story. The middle, or second act, is half of the story in length.

The structure looks like this:

Act 1: Setup

The first fourth of the manuscript introduces the main elements. Bring in the reader with a strong hook. Occasionally, the hook presents itself early in the writing, but more often a writer returns to polish the roughly crafted first chapter, the first paragraph, and the first line once the project is complete. After all, we know a lot more about the characters and plot when we've reached the end.

Begin by jumping into the action as soon as possible. Explain the details behind the excitement later. In the first act

- Bring the reader in with a strong hook

- Introduce the reader to important characters

- Present the inciting incident from which our characters have no way to return. Unable to go around, over, or under, their only way is though the story.

- Add complications and obstacles the characters we care about must face

- Provide a crisis that sets up the second act

Act 2: Confrontation

In the middle half of the manuscript the author will

- Further develop the characters

- Prevent the character we care about from achieving their goal

- Intensify the suspense

- Set up the resolution of act three with an explosive moment that has been building

Act 3: Resolution

The final fourth of the story.

- Expand the conflict to be the focal point.

- Pace the ending to feel natural and not rushed to the reader.

- Craft a satisfying ending that connects back to the beginning.

- Surprise the reader with how the details of the story come together.

- Tie up all the loose ends.

Sketching your story into the three-act template is a proven way to provide a compelling pacing. This model serves as a checklist to remind the writer to include the important ingredients of a strong plot.

Chapter Ten

Plot in Settings

As your story unfolds, use setting to tell the reader *when* and *where* they are, and how the surroundings influence the plot. See how this setting sets up the plot:

Immediately upon giving birth to her fifth child, Nelma's arms were empty. The hospital staff whisked away the baby before she could see him.

"I want to see my son," Nelma insisted.

"You need to understand, there are problems with the baby." The doctor explained that perhaps Nelma and her husband should consider an institution for their newborn.

"I want to see my son," Nelma repeated.

So the new bundle of babe was brought and placed in his mother's arms. Nelma smelled the sweet new baby smell of him; she cooed to the little boy and cradled him to her heart.

Then, ever so carefully, she unwrapped his blanket. There lay her infant, born without legs, his hands and arms not fully developed.

Nelma took it all in, caressed his soft new skin, and smiled into his trusting eyes.

"Oh," she said softly, "is that all?"

Setting is

- Time

- Place

- Surroundings

- Mood

- Cultural nuances

- Historical period

- A backdrop for a story

Craft a setting that contributes to the plot.

Chapter Eleven

Enhance Plot With Dialog

D ialog is a powerful tool for building a pivotal plot.

Of all the gin joints in the world, she walks into mine.

- Houston, we have a problem.

- You're gonna need a bigger boat.

- Help me, Obi-Wan Kenobi, you're my only hope.

- Every time a bell rings, an angel gets his wings.

- You had me at hello.

Think of how often people say one thing but mean another. Recall those situations when a speaker talks to one person while really talking to someone else.

The words a character speaks can tell the reader more than any description. For instance, when Scrooge says "Bah, humbug," those two non-words brilliantly tell the reader more about Scrooge's character than Charles Dickens could have revealed in a paragraph of description. That simple phrase immediately established the tension between Scrooge and the rest of society that celebrated Christmas. With simple dialog, the author illuminated the direction of the plot.

Dialog economically

- Reveals crucial plot points

- Shows something vital about a character

- Moves the story forward

Dialog shows a character's background, education level, emotions, motivations, nature, and prejudices. What about those shocking plot points that illicit an exclamation even from a character who is not known for using such terms?

The angel of the Lord provides a vital and life-changing plot point when the angel says to the shepherds, "Do not be afraid. I bring you good news that will cause great joy for all the people. Today in the town of David a Savior has been born to you; he is the Messiah, the Lord. This will be a sign to you: You will find a baby wrapped in cloths and lying in a manger," (Luke 2:10-12).

How a character speaks and what a character says can quickly reveal important plot points and twists.

Chapter Twelve

Write With Your Reader In Mind

As you pen your plot, keep your reader in mind.

A pivotal plot provides

- Uncertainty about the fates of the characters

- Tension

- Suspense

- Surprise

- The possibility the character the reader cares about may lose or fail

Grand master of the American action adventure novel, Clive Cussler made the New York Times bestseller list more than 20 times writing highly entertaining stories that have been published in 40 languages and in 100 countries. For this fan, I marvel at the author's bold and audacious plots.

Who are your favorite authors?

What do you like about their plot?

What do your favorite authors do in their writing craft that you want to emulate?

Chapter Thirteen

Penning Plots

Writers come in many types. Traditionally, authors work mostly as outliners, plotters, or plungers, while there are hybrids of these. While I lean to plunger, each project has its own requirements. Plots created in a historical timeline require careful planning which looks a lot like an outline.

While there are many approaches to writing, the best approach to use is the one that works for you. Most writers begin with the style that compliments their personality. With time and practice, a writer naturally creates systems and habits that serve them, their goals, and their projects.

Outliner

JK Rowling penned an outline for the fifth Harry Potter novel, *Order of the Phoenix*, on a common piece of notebook paper. Laying the page horizontal, she created a grid with the months of the school year on the left, and the plot points and significant characters listed along the top. When she had filled in the intersecting squares, Rowling knew what needed to happen in each chapter.

Plotter

Bill Myers, whose books and films sold more than eight million copies and won more than 60 national and international awards, knows where his story will go from beginning to end before he puts words on his manuscript. The author of numerous series for kids, teens, and adults, likes to use the bubble diagram technique. He described writing a seed idea onto a yellow legal pad and circling the idea. From there, Bill creates a bubble diagram, listing a variety of *what next* possibilities, followed by another level of potential plot points, and then another and another until the legal pad is filled.

With a highlighter, Myers reviews the original idea, and marks the best next event in each sequence. With this method, he maps the entirety of the story. His writing process involves following the highlighted trail on the legal pad from chapter one until 'The End.'

Plunger

My tendency is to be a plunger. *Chasing Sunrise* began as a scene that hung around my thoughts. I wrote the picture, expecting this would be a chapter in the center of the story. In the end, that first scene turned out to be the final chapter. Who knew?!

As a verbal processor, I usually don't know what I'm thinking until it comes out my mouth. Similarly, sitting at my laptop, Mac(Beth), parts of the story flow as fresh to me as they will be to the reader. Because the scenes do not appear in sequence, I write the scenes formulating in my brain. Ideas that show up later frequently reveal information that fills in earlier gaps. "No wonder the bad guy behaves in that way." When the manuscript is nearly complete, I rearrange chapters as needed for the story to make sense, add transitions, and fill in details.

Linear

Estee Zandee writes her novels sequentially from beginning to end. Taking a break once, she returned to her manuscript to discover "what the bad guy was doing while I was away." Her natural creative process is more linear.

Hybrids

Some projects organically require an author to employ a different method than their natural go-to. There is no right or wrong way to plot a story. Write your plot using the method that works for you to get the story done, or using the method the project requires to be accurate, believable, and complete.

The right way to write is the way that gets your story on paper.

Chapter Fourteen

Thank you for reading

T hank you for reading *Pivotal Plots* by P.S. Wells (PeggySue Wells) in the Quick Guide to Writing Well series *Pivotal Plots* is available in e-book and paperback.

If you have a moment, please leave a reviewon your favorite bookseller website. Reviews are the best gift you give an author.

Titles you may like by P.S. Wells include:

Quick Guides to Writing Well series
Pivotal Plots
Sensational Settings
Creative Characters
Dynamic Dialog
Point of View

Marc Wayne Adventure series
Chasing Sunrise

Check out the audio version of *Chasing Sunrise* read by Scott Hoke

The Patent

Secrecy Order

Unnatural Cause Awarded best mystery suspense of the year

Homeless for the Holidays

Check out the audio version of *Homeless for the Holidays* read by voice actor Katie Leigh

Personal Growth titles

The Ten Best Decisions A Single Mom Can Make

Slavery in the Land of the Free

The Girl Who Wore Freedom

C heck out these titles by PS Wells and PeggySue Wells

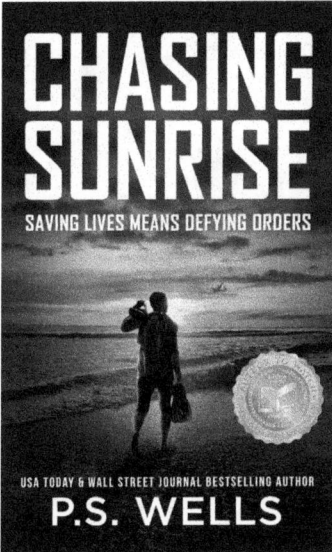

When an assignment results in a friend's death, Michael Northington seeks solace on St. Croix. When deadly players blow into St. Croix at the same time Hurricane Hugo unleashes its fury, will Michael's skills be enough to protect those he loves?

Also available in audio version, narrated by Scott Hoke.

When the world teeters on the verge of World War III, the nation that develops a patent attorney's invention will be militarily invincible in the race for global dominance. Now America's enemies have stolen the plans and kidnapped the inventor. Marc Wayne must find a way of escape before his captors realize the invention is theoretical. Or is it?

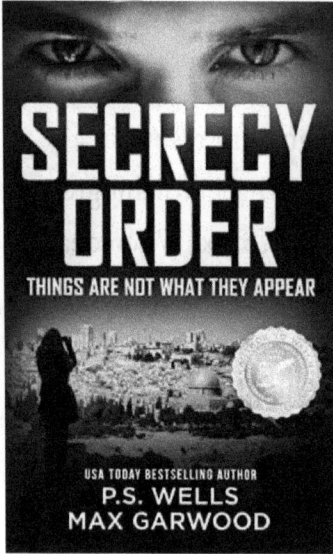

Powerful nations hunt for Marc Wayne and his invention which promises to redefine weapons and global warfare. Meanwhile, in a remote hiding place, Marc serves as bait in hopes to turn his predators into prey. When an illegal arms dealer leverages Marc for his own ends, will Marc ever see home and family again? As time runs out, can he trust the electro-physicist, Lei Quong, enough to escape with her?

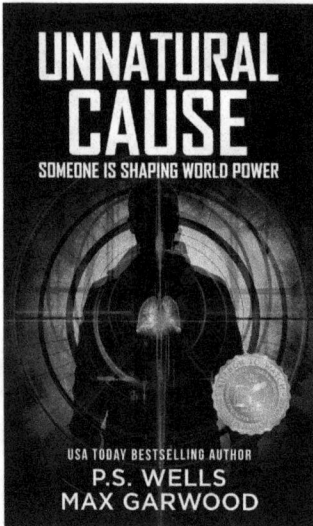

Winner of the best mystery suspense of the year, *Unnatural Cause* unpacks long unsolved family mysteries. Using a device that creates a deadly embolism from a remote location, someone is targeting world leaders to shape world power. But when Marc Wayne stops those who wield the ability to commit consequence-free murder, he finds he has played right into the mastermind's plans.

Christmas is coming, and Jack Baker's finances, friends, and future are as gone as last year's holiday. Amidst the holiday traditions and trappings, one family learns what is truly important when they lose all they have, and find they still have everything.

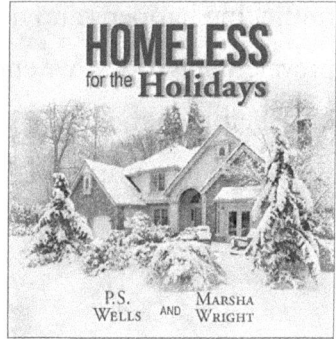

Also available in audio version read by voice actor Katie Leigh.

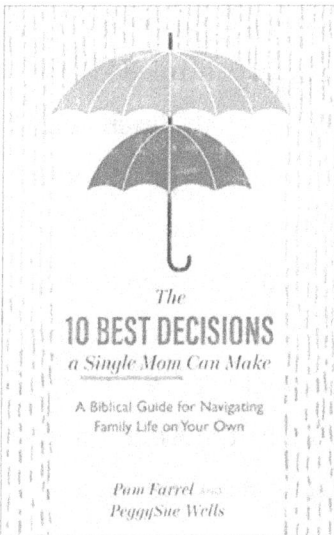

No matter how you became a single mom, you share the same challenges and fears all single moms have. How are you going to do this on your own? With humor, and sage advice, PeggySue Wells (single parent of seven children) provides practical helps and tangible tips to help you succeed.

A clear picture of how human trafficking happens and how prevalent it is today. We ended slavery once before in the United States, and we can do it again.

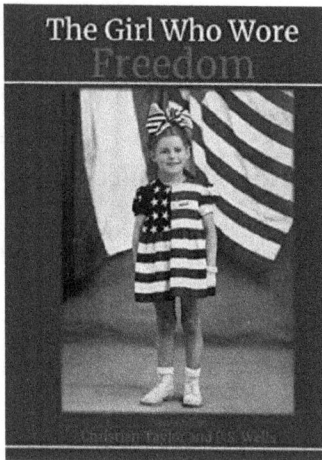

On June 6, 1944, when Dany was five years old, U.S. soldiers liberated her village from Nazi control. Soldiers established a base on Utah Beach near Dany's home, shared their provisions, and befriended the people of Sainte Marie du Mont. From the parachutes of the American soldiers who freed her, Dany's mother sewed a red, white, and blue dress resembling the American flag. Dany wore the dress at the yearly D-Day celebration and became known as *The Girl Who Wore Freedom*.

PeggySue's Particulars
to Pen

POINT OF VIEW

A Quick Guide to
Writing Well

PEGGYSUE WELLS

You want to write and write well. Point of view is the writer's most powerful tool to elicit emotion in the reader. POV can make the difference between a character appearing as a killer or a king. Learn how to pen the proper POV that compels a reader to turn pages until reaching the end.

You want to write and write well. Use this quick guide to amplify, intensify, and magnify through plot to craft a compelling story.

In this quick how-to guide, learn the particulars to craft pivotal plots that create compelling stories.

PeggySue's Particulars
to Pen

PIVOTAL PLOTS

A Quick Guide To
Writing Well

PEGGYSUE WELLS

PeggySue's Particulars
to Pen

**CREATIVE
CHARACTERS**

A Quick Guide To
Writing Well

PEGGYSUE WELLS

You want to write and write well. Use this quick guide to craft creative characters that live in the reader's mind beyond the final page of a story.

Three essentials are common to every compelling story.

1) a character the reader cares about

2) a very great life-changing, world-impacting need the character must achieve

3) a great obstacle between the character we care about and the character's life-changing, world-impacting need.

In Creative Characters, learn how to craft characters who are believable, three-dimensional, and remain in the reader's memory long after the book is read.

Stories happen in a place and that place is the setting. Settings come in four personalities.

The personalities types of setting are

- Passive

- Active

- Like a Character

- Is the Story

PeggySue's Particulars to Pen

SENSATIONAL SETTINGS

A Quick Guide To Writing Well

PEGGYSUE WELLS

What does the setting sound like, feel like, and look like? If you plan to write a book or want to improve a story, place the tale in a sensational setting. Sensational Settings: A Quick Guide to Writing Well shows you how.

PeggySue's Particulars
to Pen

**DYNAMIC
DIALOG**

A Quick Guide To
Writing Well

PEGGYSUE WELLS

Dialog is what characters say. Powerful stories are dialog-driven through carefully chosen word selections. The four purposes of dialog in your story include:

1. Move your story forward

2. Reveal something important about your plot

3. Show something important about your character

4. Give your character a unique voice

Conversations that take place between characters are often the reader's favorite part. Add value to your story by writing dialog that is clever, creative, and concise.

About the Author

P.S. Wells is a USA Today and Wall Street Journal bestselling author of 42 books (so far), and collaborator for that many more. Her novel, *Unnatural Cause* won best mystery suspense of the year.

When not writing, Wells rides horses, parasails, scuba dives, and skydives. She is the founder of SingleMomCircle.com

Connect with P.S. Wells at PeggySueWells.com

www.ingramcontent.com/pod-product-compliance
Lightning Source LLC
Chambersburg PA
CBHW060526280326
41933CB00014B/3105